Engendering Balance

A Fresh Approach To LEADERSHIP

Sue Congram, Rosie Mayes, Mary Musselbrook

Engendering Balance Publishing
www.engenderingbalance.com

Published by Engendering Balance Publishing
Dolgarren, St Weonards
HR2 8NZ
United Kingdom

Cover design, book design and graphics
Vicki Gray at Blumango Creative
www.blumangocreative.com

Kathryn Allison at IPR Communications
www.iprcommunications.co.uk

Printed and bound by Oxford University Press (UK)

British Library Cataloguing in Publication data
A catalogue record for this book is available from the British Library.

First edition
ISBN 978-0-9929958-0-5

ACKNOWLEDGEMENTS

We appreciate the generous feedback, valuable support and wise
contributions of the following people towards the development of
this book.

Shelley Adams, Kathryn Allison, Michael Carroll,
Chris Corbin, Jon Davidge, Simon Dawson, Vicki Gray,
Simon Lewis, Drew Musselbrook, Patrick Nash,
Dave Robinson, Lindsay Wittenberg.

Thank you all for helping us to bring Engendering Balance
out into the light.

CONTENTS

Creating balance offers an elegant solution to today's leadership enigma

PREFACE

Frequently, there is an abundance of rich and diverse untapped talent available to an organisation, where only a fraction of that talent is employed with the remainder overshadowed by firmly established ways of working. This gives rise to an imbalance where organisations are out-of-kilter and are not realising their potential. The corporate world has been aware, for some time, of this imbalance, yet not a lot has changed.

In this book we aim to readdress this imbalance and create a more diverse and open-book to the world of leadership. We describe how even further success can be achieved when an attitude towards engendering balance is adopted in the mindsets of leaders, managers and the workforce.

Our Story

The three of us, Sue, Rosie and Mary, first met at a gathering in 2012, for a conversation about 'seeds of new thinking in leadership' arising from Sue's PhD research which investigated the underlying dynamics of leadership. The research resonated for each of us, both personally and professionally. We had all experienced the striking, diminishing effects of being overshadowed by 'heroic' leader attitudes, as well as hearing similar stories from our clients. We also recognised occasions when each of us had overlooked valuable qualities within ourselves, acting on assumptions and beliefs of how we *should be*, rather than how we *could be*.

Our combined wealth of experience, specialisms and knowledge enriched the conversation in those early days and has resulted in establishing unique and sound roots in the philosophy, ideas and practice of Engendering Balance Ltd.

At that time Sue was in the final stages of her PhD, which is now completed. Looking back over the winding road behind her reveals over twenty-five years of working with organisations from a 'field' and systems perspective, exploring with leaders and managers how to maximise individual and collective talent. Sue had by then already published books, chapters and papers, each piece of writing offering a means for extending her own thinking and deepening her understanding and philosophy of organisational leadership. Additionally, through her research she realised the enormous contribution that women give to leadership, drawing on qualities that frequently go unrecognised. Sue believes that women can and will play an important role in shaping the future of more balanced leadership.

With the world of sport strongly shaping the road travelled behind Rosie, her equally diverse talents bring colour and character to the Engendering Balance team. With her formative life in international sport—playing netball for England, coaching the Republic of Ireland and Welsh netball teams, working as a sport scientist to the English and Welsh national rugby teams and supporting national and international, Olympic and Paralympic coaches—Rosie now links the physical, mental, emotional and spiritual performance needs of sport with leadership development. Bringing her unique wisdom to the Engendering Balance team, Rosie holds a deep felt desire to significantly influence the leadership landscape of the future.

For Mary, the road travelled to arrive at this point in the landscape had taken her through the varied terrain of business psychology and change management consultancy, into employment in industry at senior levels of management and onwards, to working independently as a leadership and team coach. Having trekked alongside private and public sector leaders and drawn deep learning from her own leadership journey, Mary brings to our triad well established capabilities for working with senior people. She is energised by supporting men and women alike to work effectively in their leadership of today's organisations.

With each of us providing rich and varied knowledge and experience to the conversation in 2012, the months ahead led to adventuring, exploring, inquiring and asking such questions as;

- Why are some living practices recognised in leadership and not others?

- Is there an essential difference between *leadership* and *leader*?

- Is the heroic model outdated and holding organisations back?

- What kind of modern-day leadership is required to best-serve organisations in today's complex world and for the future?

We now wholeheartedly believe that the full richness of leadership success can be achieved through drawing on a wider range of practices than has previously been recognised. Our research and client work has shown how people and organisations become more effective when practices, not previously associated with leadership, become recognised, valued well and encouraged. We refer to this as engendering balanced leadership, where employee core strengths are brought into practice along-side established ways of working, illuminating the whole work interaction.

In this book, we explain our thinking behind the Engendering Balance approach, what is 'eclipsed' and what needs 'illuminating', revealing a new landscape that is inspiring leaders, teams, managers and coaches to a more inclusive agenda. We lay out the foundations and thinking behind our practice and why it is important.

Using the analogy of a wave, we maintain that our approach significantly contributes to a rising surge of cutting-edge thinking in organisational leadership, where researchers and practitioners alike are on a similar course. Thus the wave is taking us beyond heroic, leader-follower mindsets, towards a more collective and inclusive proposition. What that means is, in order to succeed in today's fast paced world, many organisations have to push the boat out even further into the rocky waters. But their leaders are left with a dilemma—to stay the same, or to change?

To reach the crest of the wave means imagining what *could be* and letting go of what *should be*. The part that we play in this wave is to generate greater leadership potential throughout organisations, by illuminating qualities of practice that are eclipsed. Allowing these qualities to 'be released' can make a real difference, compelling the organisation to exceed beyond its aspirations and competitors.

We intend our approach to appeal to all those involved in leadership, leadership development, change management and inclusivity:

- Leaders at the top, who know they need to think differently to realise the potential and success of their organisations.
- Managers who want to achieve more through their leadership within the complexity of the organisations in which they work.
- Younger people stepping into leadership, or new to management, who are keen to progress.
- Enablers and coaching specialists who want to keep up with new thinking.
- Everyone who wants to make the inclusion agenda happen, to find a new angle to add to current strategies.

In this book, we describe balanced leadership, explaining the key concepts, how they have come about, where their roots lie and how you can begin to use them in your work. The position we take is accumulative, that is, not throwing away established ways of working, but building a wider range of practices to those that already exist—activities that are not yet fully alive, valued or developed. We explain how and why the capacity of individuals, teams and organisations will increase, when you embrace an attitude of inclusion to reach a new balance.

If you take from this book and implement just one new viewpoint, that's an achievement; if you take action on many, that's success.

In seeing the familiar differently the greatest changes can occur

CHAPTER 1

THE FOUNDATIONS
OF BALANCE

Imagine that you were given the freedom to develop your approach to leadership in whatever way you felt best—no longer driven by what it 'should' be, or constrained by norms, politics and convention; you could re-create it. What would leadership then look like? What purpose could it serve, for you, for the people around you and for your organisation?

Leadership is not an intellectual exercise, but a human endeavour. 'You must not confuse it with competition or control'[1] or believe that you must do it the same as others to be successful. You can imagine, choose, create a way that will achieve your success, be different because it is better and allow your wisdom to come through because it makes sense.

We live and work in a world that is out of balance or kilter. Yet, liberating ourselves from the established norm, tends not to be a priority for people in their everyday activities. In the fast track, fast thinking world of work, the main concern is to concentrate on getting results. The emotional undercurrent of this situation for many is 'if you get off the track you will get left behind'. We encourage you to stop and question, not to fear getting left behind, but to use your imagination as a springboard for leaping ahead. There are questions that we must ask ourselves, if we are to find a new balance in our workplaces and establish new practices that serve the present and the future well.

Engendering balance is imaginative, it takes a fresh approach, where leadership is located in the relational and social system of the organisation, rather than solely in the individual—the leader role is part of that system, but not all of it. This perspective adds to the bigger wave of knowledge, research and a repositioning of leadership that is arising as the pressure for a change in practice increases.

[1]'Nancy Kline (2014) p32'

The foundations of balance carry a different point-of-view. Separating leader from leadership, we offer three interconnected perspectives ranging from the individual leader, to collaborative activities, to a much broader scale of collective thinking. At the heart of our approach sit two critically important mindsets: **creating the conditions for success** and **illuminating qualities** that are currently eclipsed.

Building on this foundation, our approach offers new thinking for re-creating leadership in which individuals and organisations draw on a much greater capacity within the workforce. We explore how paradoxes and contradictions of this approach are its strength and how the interplay of a wider range of practices work together.

We set the foundations of balance by:

○ Providing a point-of-view where a core responsibility of leadership is *to create the conditions for success*;

○ Turning towards a new landscape that encourages a generative way of thinking about how leadership can achieve more, involve people more, engage creativity and grow into the future;

○ Inspiring you to draw on a wider range of practices in service to what your organisation is striving to achieve.

As you read this book we invite you to imagine our approach in the context of your own situation. Are you a CEO who wants to find solutions to complex and challenging situations? Are you a leader, heading up a division of a large corporation wanting to think differently about the future? Are you a young aspiring manager who is in that middle ground between your own imaginative thinking and traditional structures? Are you an executive coach with clients facing insurmountable problems?

Leadership is an inherent quality of the social and cultural system of an organisation

CHAPTER 2

FROM LEADER TO LEADERSHIP

Take a moment to reflect on your current team and people around you who make a difference to the success of your business, to your organisation or division, or to your area of responsibility. Imagine that they are all engaged in leadership, not as followers, but as contributors, adding vibrant and inventive value.

With this in mind, the first shifts needed to engender balanced leadership are in language and mindsets. Until now the terms leader and leadership have commonly been used interchangeably. We differentiate between them, where leader is a role and leadership arises through a wide range of actions, interactions and interventions by an equally wide range of people, including the leaders. Leadership is then seen as an inherent quality of the social and cultural system of organisations — the organisational community.

We believe that these shifts are critical in our time and for the future of organisations. Until recently, the individual-as-leader has served organisational structures fairly well. But with the economic crash, the subsequent collapse of many national and international businesses, along with the fast changing world of technology, all indicate that the role of leader as we have known it can no longer be sustained by individuals alone.

Balanced Leadership positions the individual leader role as part of the greater system of leadership within the organisation.

From this way of thinking, a valuable concern for leaders is to pay attention to the broader social system and culture of the organisation. The culture being how the values and attitudes of the organisation are embedded; the social system being visible interactions as well as hidden dynamics, of the relationships between people.

Case study: Leadership as embedded in the social system of a nursing home

The management and staff of a nursing home were proud of their compassionate values. The leadership model of the Managing Director was hierarchical, whilst at the same time he believed strongly that 'caring' was an important organisational value. The MD believed that this combination was good for a nursing home, but what he had not taken into account was how the staff were interpreting 'caring' in their behaviour between each other. Unknown to him implicit conflict-avoidance behaviours arose amongst the management and staff, resulting in his leadership becoming severely compromised—staff felt unable to speak out on issues that were going wrong, or might be taken as criticism, as a consequence resentments started building and the MD was blamed. Errors occurred in both administration and front line care for residents, quality of care declined and turnover of staff increased. The home started to lose its credibility.

Through leadership coaching with the Managing Director and the management team, action was taken to address difficult issues in a positive way. The main issue that emerged was that staff had unwittingly interpreted 'caring' as 'conflict-free', feeling concerned that anything perceived as 'not caring' would rock the boat and compromise their position. Through coaching, the MD realised that he could involve the staff more in setting values and the leadership of the home by taking into account their views, ideas and concerns. He also encouraged managers to 'take the lead' at meetings and in various situations that did not need his input. Stepping into a more balanced leadership approach, he also started listening to the views of people from within the wider social system of the home—the residents and external influences such as families of residents and the health-care system.

After a very short period, things started to improve, the MD was then able to focus on growth, rather than survival. He later shared that one of the most difficult challenges through this process was facing himself, realising that leadership is not about him having to come up with all the answers, but instead to encourage and build the best possible culture that would support the organisation's purpose and direction.

By its nature, engendering balanced leadership takes a positive and progressive position that is inclusive and collaborative, rather than individualistic and isolating. That means involving management and employees (the internal social system) and may also mean taking into consideration the broader social environment in which the organisation is positioned. As such 'the leader in their role' is only a small part of the landscape that the language of 'leadership' can fully embrace. From this standpoint, the task of a leader is to pay particular attention to the internal social system and how to **create the conditions for success.**

REFLECTIVE THOUGHTS

How easy is it for you to shift your thinking away from 'leader' towards 'leadership'? Consider why you may find this difficult. Name strengths that you already have that are aligned with leadership as described in this chapter. What is the biggest change that you would need to make within yourself and how will you achieve that?

Notes and Reflections

Success is a science; if you have
the conditions, you get the result

CHAPTER 3

CREATING THE CONDITIONS FOR SUCCESS

Put simply, organisations are a gathering of people working together, ideally with a collective purpose. Employees are the organisation. They create the vision, the structures, drive the operational systems, bring knowledge, skills and wisdom to enable success. If you reflect on your role as a leader from this standpoint, you will recognise how creating the conditions for success is about people. This is the essence of leadership today.

One of the most significant facets to our approach is in **creating the conditions for success**. Which means building a workplace environment where the best results can be achieved and replicated; a confident workplace with people who are able to contribute to leadership, have a learning attitude, feel cared about and reciprocate, along with collaborative activities that encourage and enable the people involved to learn through vital feedback. This attitude establishes respect, engenders creativity through diversity and as a consequence employees contribute more and aim higher.

In our experience it is rare for leaders to think in terms of their organisation as a whole system in this way, when they learn how to, they find it extremely valuable. On a broad scale, creating the conditions for success means cultivating the social system of the organisation—the collective contribution, imagination and relational qualities of all the people, at all levels of the system. The intention is to build an organisational community to maximise exactly why and what the organisation can potentially achieve.

As such, leadership responsibility in creating the conditions for success also means building a deeper appreciation of relational practices and networks and understanding social systems and how they function. In the nursing home case study illustrated in the previous chapter, the leader's role carried responsibility to entertain this wider challenge and to give space for the leadership capacity of the whole social system to flourish. The leader is then a contributor to creating the conditions for success—but is not the sole agent of success. One of the leader's key responsibilities is to engage participation.

Adopting a mindset of creating the conditions for success also works on an individual scale. If you step into a new role and really want to make a success of it, a good question to ask is 'What are the conditions that will help me achieve success?' and 'What do I need to change within myself?' Which may mean shifting your own personal attitude.

From this perspective, leadership can be understood as multi-dimensional and inclusive—a *gestalt* where the whole is greater than the sum of the parts.

LEADERSHIP AS A GESTALT: the whole is greater than the sum of the parts

The gestalt of leadership means that a range of sources and influences are linked together to create a whole. How leadership is experienced, or seen, depends on what is needed in the context of the immediate situation. To illustrate this we will use bird metaphors to represent three different, interconnected resources that are central to engendering balance:

- The individual perspective is represented by the **eagle**;

- The collaborative perspective is represented by **geese** flying in formation;

- The connective perspective is represented by **starlings** flocking.

EAGLE: heroic and authoritative

Imagine yourself as the eagle, the hero of the skies, holding respectful authority, with the capability of soaring high and understanding the bigger landscape. You know who you are; you carry an air of independence; standing proud in your rightful leader position. Other creatures look up to you. You work well alone, eagle-eyed, you are a survivor.

The eagle represents the role of the heroic leader as it is traditionally understood. There is an eagle in each of us, capable of speaking out, standing out, holding an authoritative voice, giving direction, knowing what is needed and getting it. The eagle establishes authority through self-knowledge, self-belief, with self-understanding, from life experiences.

Bringing the eagle position into balanced leadership means owning the eagle in yourself, as well as recognising and acknowledging eagle qualities in others. Where mutual respect exists, eagle relationships carry powerful dynamics in an organisation. The eagle then, is not always about the most senior position in the organisation. It has two important facets: the role of authority throughout the organisation and the authoritative voice of people within the organisation.

Many qualities of the eagle are needed in a variety of business scenarios. The challenge for leaders is to know the appropriateness of the eagle and to decide when other team qualities are needed, like those of geese and starlings as described below.

There is an expectation that comes with the role of a leader: that is, many people expect to be led. People do assume that the leader knows the correct direction and will convey that direction to the team. Followers then follow. This traditional belief is both compelling and seductive for those in leader roles, yet all too often it throws leadership out of balance. Yes, there are situations where a leader/follower relationship is needed, but far less than is commonly thought and understood. Many employees habitually defer to positional authority and in that moment negate their own eagle, their own authoritative voice. Habitual or fear-based deference creates imbalances in leadership, whereas mutual respect is a balancing process, irrespective of hierarchy.

We would like to stress that the authority of your own knowledge, experience, beliefs and self-understanding is powerful and cannot be underestimated. We equate personal authority with *author*-ing, that is, the capacity to write your own story, share your values, beliefs, experience, knowledge and passions, in your own unique wisdom. No-one has as much knowledge about you, as you do, so why hide it away?

Therefore, to create the conditions for leadership success means weaving your authoritative voice into the conversations at work, through sharing your knowledge, views and creative ideas with others in your team.

GEESE: collaborative and working together

Imagine yourself as a skein: geese in V formation. You work together with others to achieve your goal, drawing on a unique collaborative power to reach your target and destination. You support everyone else in your skein and they support you. You take your turn at the head of the skein and step back for others to do the same to allow conservation of energy. You call to each other as a part of keeping your formation and maintaining direction.

Where collaboration works, as in the geese metaphor, leadership arises from the combined efforts of everyone involved. There is no advantage in one person retaining the lead compared to the advantages gained through collaboration in this situation. If you think of a team in this way, everyone is working and communicating well together. Each member of the team brings their own leadership qualities to a collective process which works well.

To achieve the very best teamwork, dialogue and good collaboration are critical. Each member has to be well informed, to know what each of their team members are working on and to what capacity. Everyone has to know their role and contribution to the collaboration. Equally vital, is that each individual knows themselves well and knows the other team members enough to appreciate their collective strengths. Relationships, similarities and differences are discussed and valued, drawing on the wider strengths of the team. There has to be a realisation that not one single person carries all the strengths needed for effective leadership to occur. People are drawn less into a competitive battleground within their team and instead engage in a rich, supportive team enterprise.

To create the conditions for success for collaborative leadership means:

- Developing the capacity of a team to pool resources, support each other, value the diversity of each team member, recognise practices that are currently missing and reassess. Dependency on the team leader is replaced with interdependence between all the team or group members.

- Developing exceptional communication and mutual support so that the best possible outcomes can be achieved.

STARLINGS: flocking through connectivity

As a starling you are part of a flock made up of a very large number of birds. You have to rely on a process of connectivity within the flock. You are agile, flexible and adaptable. You can improvise and rely with assurance on your spontaneity to stay aligned. You intuitively connect with the closest starlings around you, in order to receive and transmit information and reach your goal together.

It's an amazing sight to watch the grace of starlings flocking, as the birds collectively form a dance in the sky. Flocking acts as a protection from predators; assists migration; and helps birds to maximise on food resources. The method that birds engage in this dance is by murmuration, a process of quiet connection through this bird system.

Connectivity is the key to success in this style of leadership. Flocking leadership is a process that is relational on a large scale. It's less about the hierarchical structure and more about the dynamics within the informal network of the organisational system (discussed in Chapter 7). We describe this as hidden dynamics which cannot be controlled in the same way as operational systems. Like many important leadership qualities, we believe that connectivity already exists in organisations, but is largely eclipsed and overshadowed by the prevailing leadership ethos.

Creating the conditions for success for flocking must take into account the informal functioning of the organisation, understanding what that could look like, how the qualities of good functioning can be encouraged and developed and how harmful behaviours can be changed. Success is achieved through quiet connection—listening to the hum of an organisation's social system.

COMBINING THESE THREE PERSPECTIVES:
The Eagle; The Geese; The Starlings

To know when each perspective has its place and that the other two perspectives are always close-by allows for a leaderful wisdom to emerge—to imagine, to invite, to choose creates engendering balance.

These three perspectives provide a view of leadership that can offer an added value or a contribution to any given situation, varying and shifting as the situation evolves. Together they form a gestalt, a whole picture. At any point, the eagle, the geese or the starlings, may form in different combinations to meet emerging demands. The context and relational dynamics active in each situation, determine what is most needed, creating the conditions for success. However, it also requires each member or leader to value and develop capacity to engage all three positions and to know when and how to deal with conflicting values between them when they arise.

Illustrative case study of combining the three perspectives

Working with a client who held a senior management role, her recent 360° feedback assessment revealed how team members perceived her as a leader with a strong command-and-control style. It became apparent that she viewed leadership as primarily about giving clear direction. She strongly believed it was her sole responsibility to decide on the direction, communicate this to her team and tell them how she wanted them to achieve it.

Through our coaching sessions, she recognised that in acting as an eagle leader, her strong exercising judgement could oppose the balance in her team, at certain times, quickly realising the potential consequences of such a course of action.

By adding the geese perspective to her leadership style, she initially invited one of her management team to become involved in direction-setting with her. As it turned out, this first step evolved into a reciprocal relationship, raising the confidence of both parties to then involve others in the team in a similar way. She brought into play a number of attributes that she had not previously valued in herself, in particular some important relationship capabilities.

From a flocking position, she experimented with keeping a journal about ideas/insights/information she gleaned from informal sources. She found that conversations with team members before and after meetings and in her daily interactions, surfaced valuable information. She became more attuned to what other people were thinking and feeling about team and business issues and built on these insights, successfully developing a more balanced leadership style.

What surprised this client most of all was how the team changed in response to her changing. They became more motivated, introducing new ideas to address problems that had previously seemed to her to be insurmountable. She learned how to successfully combine all three perspectives, not giving up her eagle strengths altogether, but using them appropriately and exerting choice. Her success was achieved by drawing on a much broader range of qualities of practice within herself than she had associated with leadership in the past.

REFLECTIVE THOUGHTS

We hope we have explained how to take imaginative leaps to engage in a new leadership style in this chapter. How will your understanding of these perspectives influence your actions? What one thing can you do today towards engendering balanced leadership?

Notes and Reflections

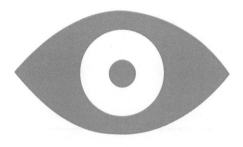

Leadership is much more of an art, a belief,
a condition of the heart, than a set of things to do.

CHAPTER 4

QUALITIES OF PRACTICE

Consider leadership as an outcome of interactions between people. When thought of in this way 'interactions' becomes the focus of attention: how to grow and develop quality relationships—between people, within teams and throughout the organisation. The language of interactions is 'relationship'. The qualities of practice are concerned with capabilities such as inclusivity, collaboration, empathy, enabling and compassion. These are not qualities that have historically been associated with leadership. We believe that now is the time to change.

In this chapter we describe how different practices contribute to leadership in a variety of ways. Central to our proposition are qualities of practice. These are ways of working that influence and shape leadership in the changing context of everyday situations. Leadership has evolved mainly through a heroic, leader-follower model—an approach that is often described as highly masculinised[2], drawing on masculinised qualities of practice and disconnected from contextual shifts and changes. Whilst historically the heroic model has been compelling, the less successful and less palatable side is also evident, the consequences of extreme hubristic behaviour in leaders[3] being one example. Nevertheless, the heroic model is highly prized and is an approach in which both men and women participate. Until recently this mindset has gone unchallenged. Changes to the global economy are now shaking the foundations of heroic leadership as a stand-alone model and demanding a more inclusive approach for the future direction of the corporate, business and political world. We believe that this inclusive perspective must now take into account qualities of practice that have not previously been acknowledged and valued within the leadership frame of reference.

We use the terms 'masculinised' and 'feminised' to categorise differences in leadership practices, in line with studies that have identified strong cultural associations with established practices and new, leading edge thinking. The following provides a few examples[4]:

[2]This is not about being male or female, but cultural and archetypal associations of masculinised and feminised ways of working that both men and women carry. See Congram (2013), Garzema & D'Antonio (2013), Koenig et al (2011).

[3]Owen (Nov. 2014)

Masculinised	Feminised
Heroic	Relational
Individualistic	Inclusive
Rational	Collaborative
Deterministic	Connective
Structured	Enabling
Task Driven	Nurturing
Objective	Imaginative
Analytical	Inquiring
Discriminate	Intuitive
Logical	Flexible
Directive	Responsive
Decisive	Adaptable
Linear	Approachable

We want to emphasise that men and women embody qualities from both the masculine and the feminine categories. The salient point is that in leadership many feminine qualities become eclipsed in favour of masculinised practices, by both men and women. This can occur both inside and outside—how a person chooses to act and how a person is impacted by others and the environment around them. An excellent example can be drawn from the 1980's and '90's period when assertiveness training became popular. Focusing on the masculinised quality, many people discovered they could apply and become successful managers and leaders. Regrettably and with a huge dollop of hindsight, the methods used in most assertiveness training meant the loss or lack of feminine qualities being taught and conveyed, such as inclusivity and empathy. Thereby leaders of the day were without balancing qualities, appearing harsh, outspoken, pushy or controlling. Whilst we recognise there are times when greater assertion is needed, we invite you to consider the desired outcomes, in exerting choice through balanced action. To

[4] Examples are drawn from a much wider list that researchers have identified: Congram (2013); Garzema & D'Antonio (2013); Koenig, et al. (2011).

note, neither category is good or bad, but should be considered as aspects in each of us that carry valuable leadership qualities. Our ability to draw on these qualities, in ourselves and in others, is a great strength. The few people who do this are often held up as renowned leaders.

Disappointingly, these terms are often confused with the language of 'men' and 'women', leading to strong reactions. Although these reactions interfere with learning balanced leadership, we believe they are worth exploring as part of the new leadership challenge—where prejudices and deep assumptions can be brought into awareness and questioned. This is a concern which has to be addressed if balance is to be achieved. Other terms that point towards similar differences have been suggested to us, such as 'soft and hard', 'left brain and right brain', 'operational and people'. In our view these terms do not carry the depth of understanding needed for sustainable change. The value of maintaining the masculine-feminine language and overcoming inhibiting prejudices, means that leaders recognise qualities that already exist within themselves, but perhaps did not previously value. For many, this process is both liberating and re-balancing, leading to a much greater potential leadership style.

What does this mean for engendering balanced leadership?

The supremacy of masculinised leadership does make it hard to change. Heroic leaders (the eagle) are deterministic, directive, decisive and use authoritative practices in their leadership style. This, if not recognised, can quickly overshadow qualities of feminised leadership. We need both masculinised and feminised ways of working, for the healthy functioning of collaborative (geese) and connective (starlings) leadership. For instance, with direction and purpose, both collaboration and connectivity call for nurturing, empathy and relationship-building to function incredibly well within the geese V formation or starling flocking. Where these practices are acknowledged and valued, wise choices for action and interaction can be made and balance achieved. We recognise that the eagle, geese and starling positions require different measures of masculine (Mm) and feminine (Ff) qualities[5], expressed as: Eagle **Mf,** Geese **mf,** Starlings **Fm**, demonstrating how the overall tone needs to change to readdress the balance.

The question then is: Are there differences between men and women when striving for balanced leadership? The nature-nurture debate means that the jury is out on that question. Nevertheless a simple way of looking at it is through identity. A man may identify with cultural associations of authority and competitiveness, whilst he can also be enabling and nurturing. Equally, women have demonstrated their authoritative and competitive side, whilst at the same time drawing on qualities that sit deeply within (are culturally nurtured) and linked to their feminine identity.

Influencing change when the old roots are deep is not an easy process. The provision of leadership development is in a position to deliver this change, yet people in professions concerned with recruiting, assessing and developing leaders are caught up as much in cultural traditions as their clients. In addition, only recently discovered is a mischievous rogue beneath the surface of heroic leadership called unconscious bias[6], striving to keep things the same. New leadership development requires imagination and the courage to change—to illuminate eclipsed practices and raise awareness of underlying forces that get in the way. Balance can be achieved by men and women alike, drawing on the full range of qualities of the masculine and the feminine, but this shift does need a shift in mindsets:

[5] Where M=high proportion of masculine qualities, m=some masculine qualities, F=high proportion of feminine qualities, f=some feminine qualities.
[6] For more information on this topic look at Kandola (2009).

▷ We believe that culturally established beliefs can and must be challenged in the face of leadership.

▷ We believe that men and women alike are capable of living all the qualities needed to bring leadership into balance.

REFLECTIVE THOUGHTS

In your leader role, how do you respond to the language of masculine and feminine as definitions of qualities of practice? How do you think others will respond? If you feel uncomfortable in any way with this language, what is that discomfort about? What do you need to do to overcome any fears and concerns associated with these words and their meanings, for you, for others and for the business or organisation?

Notes and Reflections

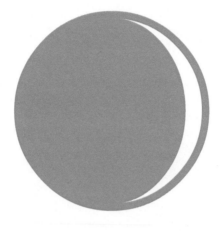

People are like stained-glass windows.
Their true beauty is revealed only if there is
a light from within.

CHAPTER 5

FROM ECLIPSING
TO ILLUMINATING

Eclipsing is the obscuring of the light from one object by the passing of another object between it and its source of illumination, such as in a solar or lunar eclipse.

UNDERSTANDING WHAT IS ECLIPSED

In our studies, we have concluded that the dominance of the leader-as-hero model creates an eclipse[7], overshadowing practices that would otherwise serve leadership well and therefore setting up an imbalance in the way that organisations operate. Further investigations revealed that this occurrence was not intentional and just not understood. In addition, during our research we observed that eclipsing stems from both external and internal processes:

- **Externally** people become eclipsed by others and by the system in which they work. For example, their organisation may reward and value some ways of working more than others, which the workforce then conform to, rather than challenge. Performance management systems are frequently part of the problem when they could be part of the solution.

- **Internally** you may unknowingly eclipse aspects of yourself through overvaluing other qualities. For example, recognising personal unconscious prejudices against 'soft skills' in favour of valued 'hard skills' allows for a change in thought and action, creating an opening to illuminate the 'soft skills' in conjunction with the 'hard skills' to balance leadership style.

In many organisations qualities that have become eclipsed are critical for building cohesion between people and generating collective belonging. Without this an organisation is not strong, creative, or productive. In a few organisations, the reverse is true, the need to establish and maintain an organisational community that carries a sense of family and belonging, can eclipse decisive action and clear direction.

[7]See Congram 2013

Illuminating eclipsed practices is more of an awareness-raising process than knowledgeable input and therefore is transformative. Where internal eclipsing is self-limiting, the process of illuminating becomes liberating.

ILLUMINATING: FROM SURVIVING TO THRIVING

To illuminate means to 'shine a light from within, or to shine a light onto'. We believe that both are needed. As the famous quote by Marian Williamson succinctly describes:

'And as we let our own light shine,
We unconsciously give other people permission to do the same.'

To recognise and value eclipsed practices means illuminating what is being eclipsed—bringing out of the shadow into the light. As we have already indicated, that does not mean diminishing the body of practices that cause the eclipse, on the contrary, these need to continue to be valued. Instead what happens is that established practices naturally shift (rather than a controlled shift), in relation to new practices coming into view and being valued. For instance, authoritative leadership styles continue to be valued and relevant, but shift in their dominance when collaborative practices become illuminated. One way of understanding this process metaphorically is through colour. Let's assume that authoritative leadership is red. On a white background red is a strong dominant colour.

When blue is brought alongside the red, our perception of red changes, it is complemented by the blue—not dominated by it. They co-exist and work well together.

Add a further colour and the whole image changes, the combination becomes even more interesting with not one of the colours dominating.

If these primary colours represent the three leadership perspectives of eagle, geese and starlings, then metaphorically what we see is the possibility that they can all live and work well together. Although the reality of this is more complex, it demonstrates the need for balance and how balance shifts according to which colours are illuminated. Translated into a leadership example, the balance shifts when collaboration is illuminated with equal light alongside individual leadership.

ILLUMINATING THE INNER AND THE OUTER

Shining a light from within, means acknowledging and valuing your own talents and qualities, making them visible for others to see. Although personal habits and patterns can lead people to self-eclipse, as we have explained, cultural beliefs and attitudes can also lead to eclipsing. That is, the extent that you hold back on some qualities within yourself in favour of others, because of culturally learned beliefs. One way of explaining this is to consider yourself in each of the bird illustrations:

The eagle qualities are about illuminating your authority, decisiveness and discernment, your ability to articulate clarity when things are confusing, to stand out and be seen. By way of example, our work with clients has shown the extent that many people eclipse their own personal authority through their role authority. We believe that the power of personal authority is a greater strength than the role, working with the client to illuminate this in themselves and living it to the full.

The geese qualities are to do with being part of a team, working together in formation, illuminating your collaborative values and capabilities and not holding back. Appreciating your own diverse qualities, in relation to others, whilst also owning and showing your vulnerability will lead to being included and inclusive, enabling and empathetic to playing an active role in a team. Expanding awareness is an important part of this process. The qualities described are frequently eclipsed by eagle qualities within. They are not valued in the same way and often treated disparagingly as 'soft skills'.

The starling qualities, means recognising your part in the wider social system of the organisation, feeling connected and valuing your connections with others. Taking the initiative to talk with people you know, as well as getting to know others, holding a sense of enquiry; both finding out and feeding into the network. Flocking qualities mean being mindful of others, tuning into the bigger conversation, bringing your own caring self to the system and contributing to a healthy network.

Blame cultures are not healthy systems as employees often collude, rather than deal with the issues behind the blame. Illuminating from within these can mean recognising and dealing effectively with your own grumblings before they spiral out of control. Strong self-belief is an excellent support for illuminating qualities that have become eclipsed from within.

Shining a light on others is about bringing awareness to the eclipsed talents and qualities in others, so that they too can be acknowledged and valued.

We often find in our work that people have an attitude towards learning based on deficit thinking. Engendering balance is different in that people have many qualities within them that have become eclipsed, sometimes beyond recognition. Knowing what is being eclipsed is the first step to illuminating. We believe leadership learning and development can usefully guide managers and leaders towards shining a light on the eclipsed qualities of others and a balanced leadership for the organisation.

REFLECTIVE THOUGHTS

The eagle How often do you openly acknowledge others for their ability to stand in their authority, to make good decisions, to articulate direction with clarity? How often do you show your appreciation to people above you when they illuminate qualities not previously so evident? As many of you reading this book will know from your own personal experience, leading from the top is a lonely place. To be acknowledged is affirming and makes that place less lonely.

The geese What does it mean to illuminate qualities that have been eclipsed and yet are at the heart of working together collaboratively? We believe that drawing attention to collaborative strengths, is one way of doing this. For example, a leadership team that Sue worked with could not establish effective team alignment (a skein). She noticed that they were very quick to voice each other's personal weaknesses and their weaknesses as a team, but repeatedly failed to acknowledge their strengths. Instead of pointing this out—which could have been taken as yet another weakness—Sue illuminated eclipsed qualities by acknowledging behaviours and activities that were supportive of collaboration, illustrating how they could value these behaviours as and when they occurred in the business setting. The team soon realised that they had a lot more going for them than had been previously recognised. Sue's interventions led them to positively align themselves with each other and to shift their balance of team leadership.

The starlings How often do you let others know that their relationship-building strengths are invaluable to the organisation? These qualities that build a strong community within the organisation are critical to an organisation's success. Shedding a light on connective practices means encouraging people to give voice to things that matter—and letting them know that they have been heard. It is about acknowledging the relational strengths in leadership, as well as illuminating the qualities that keep the connective processes healthy and valuable to balanced leadership.

The experience of illuminating is liberating. It's not about a need for new knowledge, but how you bring your own and other people's eclipsed qualities to life, inwardly and outwardly. To do this may involve questioning your personal assumptions, biases and habitual thinking, as well as the organisation's cultural beliefs about leadership and how success is achieved. Our approach in our work is to encourage individuals and teams to recognise what is effective about what you do, then to do it more. Although this may seem paradoxical, we recognise that problems and issues can consume attention in such a way that what is good, supportive and functional, becomes overshadowed by what is dysfunctional.

Do you shine in your leadership, illuminating your own strengths as well as those of others? Or is there a part of you that is eclipsed? How can you begin to shine a light on all of your qualities and step more fully into your leadership capacity?

Thinking the same keeps you in the past,
thinking differently takes you into the future.

So far we have described the main concepts behind the engendering balanced leadership idea. You may wish to take a moment to reflect on what more you could achieve by valuing a much broader range of qualities of practice within yourself and in others, to increase leadership success.

The rest of this book describes: living the balanced leadership approach; the formal and informal systems of organisations and why they are important; becoming aware of the impact of different depths of learning; how to become a role model for others. A final short chapter brings attention to the futuristic nature of engendering balanced leadership.

Notes and Reflections

The sun rises each morning to shed light
on the things we may have overlooked the day before

CHAPTER 6

LIVING THE BALANCED LEADERSHIP APPROACH

What goes unnoticed is not unreal. **The choices you make and those of which you are not mindful, still exist, influencing your actions and interactions as you go about your daily life. How do you consciously make moment-by-moment decisions as you navigate your way through each day—in meetings, in your networks, in your work, in your relationship with others? These are not the big business decisions, but the choices that fill out micro-moments of interaction and affect the balance of your leadership. Many of these choices go unnoticed until you actually pay some attention. They exist in your decisions to act and how you act. These choices are usually habitual, influenced by belief systems, unconscious bias[8] and shaped by the deep roots of your cultural values. They steer your leadership out of balance and therefore can also steer you towards balance.**

Making choices for balanced leadership includes drawing on the full range of masculinised and feminised ways of working. There is a skill and art in bringing these two rich seams into lively inter-play.

WHAT BALANCED LEADERSHIP COULD LOOK LIKE

One challenge that accompanies balance is bringing together ways of working that seem to be in contradiction. Many qualities work well together, but in the first instance it can appear that some do not. Context (C) is also vitally important—to take qualities of practice out of context defeats the point that we are making. The following examples illustrate how combining masculine and feminine qualities can work. They are set in typical leadership situations, but as the context of everyday is situationally different, these are illustrative rather than prescriptive.

[8]See Kandola (2009)

Heroic and Relational

The CEO and founder of a small business of fifty
employees was a proud man and had always led
from a strong leader-follower attitude. Working with
him meant coaching him to strengthen his perception
of himself as a leader, as well as illuminating his
relational, more feminised qualities, which he then
used to pull his business out of crisis.

The story of the CEO came to a head during the
economic downturn, the business fell into debt,
customers were not paying on time combined with a
fifty percent reduction in orders. The CEO attempted
to come up with the answers on his own 'to lead the
business out of crisis', without much success. At that
point he asked for help.

The foremost challenge for him was to face himself,
particularly his pride. He believed that talking to any
of the employees about the trouble the business was
in, was deemed to himself to be a failure. This belief
was self-defeating and business limiting, an attitude
that in-depth coaching was able to work through with
him. Whilst going through an intense self-reflective
coaching programme, he was also invited to consider
leadership from a much broader viewpoint. This
meant drawing out relational qualities that he carried
but had not previously associated with leadership. For
example, when asked 'What really matters to you?',
he showed great compassion towards people in the
world who he described as 'suffering'—a quality that
turned out to be valuable in pulling the business out

of crisis. Other relational qualities were identified
through the narratives in his coaching. He was then
able to use a range of these qualities (strengths) to
'turn his business around' and to value them in his
leadership.

The CEO started to involve management and staff—
instead of leading with answers he led with the crisis,
sharing a very real problem. Decisions were taken
collectively, with all employees involved. One of those
decisions being for all staff to take a temporary cut in
wages as a way of financially rescuing the business
and avoiding redundancies—a path that the CEO had
not previously considered. The business survived,
eventually becoming more successful than before the
crisis. Paradoxically, the CEO was seen as a hero for
approaching the crisis in this way.

More traditional coaching approaches might have challenged the
CEO on his strong heroic style. Rather than do that, our approach
was (and is) to illuminate and value qualities of practice for building
relationships and connectivity within the organisation. We believe that
insights and advantages gained through illuminating qualities and
putting them into practice appropriately, have a balancing effect.

Directive and enabling

The IT company was losing ground against their
competitors in a fast growing market, something had to
change if they were to survive. Working with the
executive team led to them growing a much better

understanding of each other and realising how they could achieve the best out of the organisation by developing 'a community of practice'[9]—an organisation of ideas and learning. To do this they needed a strong sense of purpose for the organisation, in Simon Sinek's[10] terms, starting with 'WHY'; why the business existed, its unique purpose in the market of IT. They also initiated a complete change of the company's appraisal system in favour of a more enabling, inclusive and conversational process.

The company had previously established a directive style in their management and leadership. People had been recruited for their specialist IT skills, whilst performance management systems provided direction on how to utilise those skills in the operations of the business. The focus was on technical capability, people skills had not been considered other than in the Human Resources department. All employees had an annual appraisal, largely focusing on the contribution of technical expertise to the business—a formal, structured process administered by managers, which, we later found out, was immensely disliked.

The executive team coaching focused on balanced leadership. The team identified six of their most predominant practices; directive, decisive, structured, logical, visionary and relational. Realising this way of working to be out of balance, the team decided to adopt a more enabling attitude, whilst still holding authority over the direction of the business. Our approach to this being to identify and value the

[9]Communities of practice are groups of people who share a concern or a passion for something they do and learn how to do it better.

[10]Simon Sinek TED talk (2009) http://go.ted.com/uYK

more 'feminised' qualities that we observed in them, then coach them to role model dialogic (rather than monologic)[11] leadership practices—engaging in two-way dialogue that is generative, enabling and inclusive. Carrying out appraisals was a particular task where they could put this approach into action, starting with their senior management team.

The role modelling of balanced leadership, along with a change in the appraisal system, led to fundamental shifts within the organisation, opening up opportunities and enabling employees at all levels to take initiatives and grow ideas.

Authoritative and Inclusive

A leadership team headed up the overseas division of an international manufacturing company: the team consisted of six people, five men and a woman. Through Leadership Team Coaching they discovered that their strong desire to work well together was eclipsing their personal and collective authority. They feared losing their close bonding if they opposed each-others' opinions in any way, although this concern had never been voiced.

The team had been working together for over a year and were proud of their inclusive style; a quality that was part of their valued identity. As much as they appreciated each other's contributions, they could not understand why they were not achieving the results that they believed were possible. To discover what

[11]See Scharmer (2009)

might be going on they agreed to be observed in-action and for the observer to give immediate feedback to the team as they noticed something taking place that could be throwing the team off-balance. The team were able to see their own behaviours in context and in real time.

The coach observed that each individual authoritative voice became eclipsed by the need to include others. Important insights were lost and decisions not made at a pace that served the division well. With this new information, each member of the team learned how to voice their authority (take up an eagle position) whilst at the same time preserve their valued identity. For example, the Head of Operations started to voice her opinion a lot more 'My view is that we need to make a decision today, not wait until tomorrow. I don't think that all of you will agree with that view, but I believe an early decision now will give us more time later' — a statement of both authority and inclusivity.

Coaching the team in-action brought this assumption to the surface, resulting in the team learning how to weave together authority with inclusivity. The team's performance improved reaching levels that they had always believed they could achieve.

Engendering balanced leadership is different in every situation, there is not a recipe or a formula that can tell people how to achieve it. There are instead three guides:

- the principles of the masculine and feminine qualities of practice;

○ the leadership perspectives of eagle, geese and starlings, which takes into consideration both formal and informal organisational systems discussed in the next chapter;

○ an attitude of creating the conditions for success.

With these in mind balance can be achieved to meet the needs of any situation.

REFLECTIVE THOUGHTS

Consider your work schedule, meetings and activities in the week ahead.
When would it be most beneficial to draw on your heroic and relational qualities at the same time?
Is there a situation or setting you can test being both directive and enabling practices?
Where, how and when can you combine both authoritative and inclusive qualities to achieve a great result?

Notes and Reflections

The dynamics that underlie social interaction
need to be accounted for

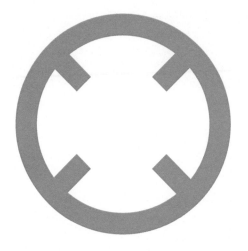

CHAPTER 7

FORMAL AND INFORMAL SYSTEMS

Think of how you go about your daily life, for instance do you arrive at work on a Monday morning highly task focused, thinking only about what you need to achieve in your day? Or are you more excited about what people did over the weekend, engaging in conversation around the coffee machine? Perhaps you started this process on the way to work, sending text messages, or making phone calls. With this in mind, your leadership involves two systems: the formal system — the hierarchical structure — and the informal system, which we also refer to as the organisational community.

The organisational community is a far more informal, fluid system and equally as powerful as the formal hierarchy of the organisation. This informal system is the heart of an organisation, the living and breathing life-force where people engage in meaningful work together, creating a sense of belonging, self-worth and identity. As well as providing people with salaried incomes, the workplace also offers a means for fulfilling deep human needs — learning, professional growth, engaging in meaningful work, being part of something bigger to be proud of, achieving collective success. And for many, contributing to a better society.

What we have found is that the need for understanding and growing the informal system, is frequently overshadowed by the hierarchical structures and operational focus. There are people and there are functions and operations created by people. Focusing on the hierarchical acts like a magnet, drawing attention towards tasks, actions, results, performance and away from people, relationships and the organisational community. When this happens important information is missed, both good and bad; where excitement is growing, opportunities to build on are missed; where pockets of creativity form, the chance to develop these does not materialise. Typically, when rewards are heavily weighted towards operations and performance within the formal system, without recognition of the more human aspects of work life, symptoms arise, such as blame, negativity, employee dissatisfaction. Using the bird metaphor, this happens through starling behaviour as quiet murmurings—and sometimes not so quiet.

Balanced leadership pays equal attention to both the formal and informal systems, with equal value.

FORMAL AND INFORMAL SYSTEMS EXPLAINED

Just as hierarchies are business critical, so are informal systems. Leadership has traditionally focused on the formal system, not fully appreciating the value of informal systems and taking responsibility for creating conditions within the informal system that are advantageous. With most organisations the informal system is powerful and influential in achieving results. From a balanced leadership perspective, the informal system is the main source of connectivity—starling activity. Creating the conditions for success means ensuring a healthy and supportive informal system. For example, blame cultures often occur because of lack of communication between management and staff, or highly controlling formal systems. Yet gossip cannot be controlled, it is a characteristic of the fluidity of the informal system and may be a symptom of an organisation that is out of balance. When this is the case, opening channels between the formal and informal systems becomes necessary, which could mean inviting staff to management meetings, or leaders spending more time with staff, listening to their concerns and their ideas and acting on them.

Leadership therefore means making choices about how both systems can best serve the business, ensuring a good flow of communication between the two and maintaining a healthy and supportive informal system. It is a responsibility of leaders to ensure that open channels of communication exist between the formal and the informal systems, flowing both ways. It is also a necessary skill or ability to be able to step back and take a look at the bigger social system of the organisation, asking such questions as; 'Is it healthy?', 'Does it function in service to the business?', 'Does it undermine what the business is aspiring to achieve?', 'Are there grumblings that need to be listened to?'. If there is toxicity in the system, management may be responsible for intervening (and not colluding with it), with leaders also asking 'what is missing?'.

REVEALING THE UNSPOKEN

There are a number of clichés that indicate hidden issues and emotions in organisations, such as 'the elephant in the room', 'the hippopotamus in the corner'. Notably these are not small issues, but an accumulation of unspoken voices and concerns that are not being dealt with. Everybody acknowledges, but nobody knows how to deal with it, neither in the formal or in the informal systems of the organisation. Such dynamics[12] can be incredibly disruptive to both the functioning of the organisation and of relationships between people.

Hidden issues often get avoided for two reasons;
1   They are deemed as too difficult to deal with
2   They cannot be controlled.

For instance, you might want a team to operate in a certain way, but you cannot make that team enjoy doing it, or stop them feeling irritated by your insistence.

An example of hidden dynamics is unconscious bias, mentioned in Chapter 4, which, if not dealt with, will throw an organisation out of balance. Leaders' who are driven by their own unconscious bias, whether culturally or individually, make decisions based on their biased thinking—until such biases are brought into awareness nothing changes. The potential of an organisation will continue to be diminished by it and leadership stymied.

[12]This process as often referred to as a 'dynamic field', a term that originated in the social sciences (Lewin 1943, Cooper 1976, Bourdieu 1992)

Managing hidden dynamics is achieved through reflection, awareness and voicing what is, as well as how it is, not through control. Consequently, learning how to engender balanced leadership carries a strong and powerful focus on reflective practice and awareness raising activities, that means learning more about what lies beneath the surface of the relational and social system—learning in depth. As a result, leaders become better informed of hidden forces that shape the way people respond and act to situations, both formally and informally. They learn how to encourage and facilitate a healthy social system, of which they too are a part. They discover how to benefit from that social system in their leadership and the value that their own role modelling can add (see Chapter 9).

REFLECTIVE THOUGHTS

The qualities of connectivity help us tune into the informal system. Leaders can draw on their capacity to listen more deeply to conversations and pay greater attention to their teams on arrival at work until home-time. Imagine what results can be achieved when the informal system is up-beat and alive.

Who do you need to listen to more?
What do you observe and therefore what do you need to ask about?
What would it take for you to tune into the informal system more?

Human resources are like natural resources;
they're often buried deep

CHAPTER 8

DEPTHS OF LEARNING

We believe that for useful leadership development to take place both rational and emotional learning is necessary. To make the transformative shifts needed for balance, means reaching into deeper layers that are fundamental to the way that people shape and give meaning to leadership.

To grow leadership means developing different kinds of learning—balance cannot be achieved just through redefining skills, styles and behaviours. Experience tells us that different learning and development takes place at different behavioural and psychological depths. These different depths are currently not well attended to in many leadership development agendas. We believe that introducing the notion of balance to the heart of learning is now vitally important: to ensure organisations can face the challenges of the twenty-first century and more importantly to grasp new opportunities.

LAYERS OF LEARNING

As explained throughout this book, engendering balanced leadership is different in that learning is predominantly aimed at drawing out, or illuminating eclipsed qualities of practice. Knowledge, skills and techniques then support the expansion and integration of new awareness.

A key focus for balanced leadership, is on learning how to illuminate eclipsed practices in the individual, team and throughout the organisation. We believe that to do this effectively requires an ability to work in-depth. We use the analogy of a tree to explain what we mean by 'depth' through layers that are interconnected and dynamic, rather than static and fixed. The layers are: (1) above the surface (2) just beneath the surface (3) the deep roots.

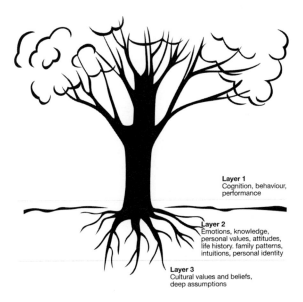

Layer 1
Cognition, behaviour, performance

Layer 2
Emotions, knowledge, personal values, attitudes, life history. family patterns, intuitions, personal identity

Layer 3
Cultural values and beliefs, deep assumptions

THE FIRST LAYER, above the surface, is the tree itself, open to the environment, visible and easy to describe as it changes over time in relation to the weather and the seasons. As an analogy for learning, this layer provides observable phenomena:

actions and behaviours

cognition

performance

what is said and how it is said

how a person presents themselves

how others respond

Examples of learning and practice in this layer, include performance management systems, professional skills and competencies and behavioural learning such as assertiveness training. This layer carries strong rationality and logic. It is an important layer for that reason—rationality is familiar to us—but without deeper insights and awareness, both coaching and leadership development can feel dry and lifeless.

THE SECOND LAYER, beneath the surface, is at a critical point where the roots meet the tree, acting as a life source for the tree. In terms of learning, this layer cannot be directly seen but is vital. Life here is not separate from that above the surface, but in a world where the value of rational thinking is seen as greater than emotional well-being, this layer can appear less important. Here exist many aspects of life that are not generally in awareness day-to-day, unless called upon, such as: emotions, knowledge, personal values and attitudes, life history, family patterns, longings, thoughts, intuitions, personal identity and many more. Leadership learning at this depth concerns awareness raising, strengthening emotional capabilities, reflective practice and hidden relational dynamics.

In recent years leadership learning has taken an enormously beneficial turn, initiated by Daniel Goleman through Emotional Intelligence[13]. He provided an acceptable language that has inspired imagination, leading to a growing wave of new thinking. Learning within this layer calls for a certain amount of reflective practice and self-awareness. There is a growing acknowledgement today of the advantages to leadership when leaders and managers embark on learning that deepens self-awareness.

THE THIRD LAYER, the deep roots of the tree, is far less accessible. These roots have two specific functions, to nourish the tree with nutrients and water and to keep it stable and in balance. This layer is rarely considered in leadership learning. Yet, just as the tree cannot survive and flourish without its deeper roots, so too, people all over the world draw on their roots in everyday interactions—our cultural values and beliefs, deep assumptions and aspects of life that we all take for granted.

This depth acknowledges that we are restricted by our established belief system and the biases and filters through which we interpret the world. As such, there are no absolute truths, only different

[13]Goleman (1995)

perspectives. Ingrained habits, attitudes and taken-for-granted beliefs can stop us from seeing other perspectives and that success could be achieved in different ways. Leadership is a typical example where the past is deeply entrenched in cultural attitudes, where the heroic model is symbolic of what many believe successful leadership to be. Balance calls for deep shifts to take place in the way that people think about, understand and embody leadership.

Learning at this depth is transformative[14] resulting in significant change of habitual patterns, towards fundamental shifts in thinking and in practice. Again, this calls for a different approach to learning and development compared to the first two layers. Here the use of metaphor and symbolism typically provide useful vehicles for attaining deep shifts in attitudes and beliefs. For example, with our everyday language full of metaphor, this can be used as a creative and imaginative way for working in-depth. When someone keeps referring to the 'flow of her life', then that is a metaphorical statement that will hold personal meaning and is likely to be rooted in the deeper layers.

One-to-one and team leadership development within the engendering balance framework offers transformative learning because it connects with these deep roots. With the right vehicle for learning, such as metaphor, narrative, art-based, or a lens that amplifies the oddities of cultural behaviour, it is possible to gain transformative insights quickly and safely. The engendering balance approach is to connect with the deeper layers, then bring insights gained into open conversation—in this way individuals and teams find their own way through the cultural maze of leadership. They discover and make choices over what is habitual and taken for granted. They retain what is valuable in the old and add what is illuminated in the new.

[14]Mezirow (1991)

In our experience achieving balanced leadership means making transformative shifts in attitudes, particularly concerning deeply embedded beliefs. The learning methods to achieve this must be able to connect with the deepest layer of the roots. With specialised training and application, coaching can offer transformative learning for the individual. Experience also tells us that team and small group coaching, offers an ideal structure to explore and inquire in-depth, to raise awareness of taken-for-granted habits that no longer serve leadership well. If those in leader roles are to take up the mantle to role-model balance, then we believe that learning in-depth is an essential part of that process.

REFLECTIVE THOUGHTS

In your own learning, how often do you reflect at layer three? When you do, what kinds of questions challenge you? What is THE BIG question that calls to you, the one that will not go away? You know it's a big question because it's uncomfortable and doesn't sit well, but has to be addressed to achieve engendering balance.

Notes and Reflections

Example is not the main thing in influencing others.
It is the only thing.

CHAPTER 9

LEADERSHIP AS
ROLE MODEL LEARNING

In the evolution of life, you learn from role models and you become a role model—both are relevant. When there are no immediate role models to help you to understand and develop a leadership style with a different approach, then the way forward becomes a testing ground for finding out. You learn and become the role model for others. For that you will need an open mind, imagination, a willingness to try new things out, to tolerate your mistakes and a sharp wit to navigate around the blocks that cross your path!

It transpires that role model learning has far more impact than a large number of leadership development programmes[15]. This poses a question—how do new practices begin, when there are no role models to demonstrate? For example, clients and people we know have said to us that role models are lacking when it comes to balanced leadership and have asked 'Where do I look to see how this works?'. We believe that role models are critical to establishing balance and yet leaders today are presented with an unusual challenge—how to learn when there are few people to show the way.

ROLE MODELS AS A SOURCE OF LEARNING

Role model learning is one of the hidden dynamics of organisational systems. You never know when it is happening or what is being learned. We are not talking about people who are held up as heroes, or seeking out a perfect example of someone who exhibits a set of standards and values. Whilst many who carry authority, status and/ or influence are highly likely to be role models (positive or negative), others have yet to realise that their behaviour, actions and values are a source of learning for others and by others—a leadership responsibility.

People take a lead from leaders (whether eagle, geese or starlings) often without being aware, in return this action will influence others. However, when learning is gained through role models from the

[15]Role modelling is an everyday reality where learning from others in organisations is pervasive (Congram 2013, Sealy 2008)

past, such as a parent or significant adult, then traditional practices, whilst necessary, are more likely to continue with change reduced to a snail's pace. This can be demonstrated, in today's world, with the slower than expected rise in the number of women in senior positions. At this time, role models who exhibit balance are few and far between. We believe that an awareness of and attention to day-to-day role model learning is a vital source of learning for growing balanced leadership.

BECOMING A ROLE MODEL

How do you develop your leadership when there is no-one to learn from?

We believe there is a challenging leap that can be achieved, with the right learning support. We encourage the notion of a testing ground, adding individualistic (eagle), collaborative (geese) and collective (starlings) role modelling practices, in a balanced way. We encourage role model learning through smaller groups, where group members can support each other, discuss and explore the challenges that they face and safely express ideas and concerns. Reflecting deeply as a group into culturally established practices, you are able to share and overcome challenges through an exploratory and inquiring attitude. In this environment you are encouraged to think differently by:

- **Shifting** attitudes from leader to leadership.
- **Reflecting** individually and collectively on practices that eclipse.
- **Illuminating** and valuing eclipsed practices in yourself and in others.
- **Discovering** how to live balanced leadership that will inspire others.

REFLECTIVE THOUGHTS

As a role model you will never know quite what other people are learning from you. The question is, what would you like them to learn and how does that make a difference to the way that you lead and engage in leadership?

Notes and Reflections

We have a responsibility in our time,
not to be prisoners of history, but to shape history

CHAPTER 10

SHAPING THE FUTURE

Creating balance offers an elegant solution to today's leadership enigma, illuminating the eclipsed, calling on both masculine and feminine qualities, attending to the eagle, geese and starlings responsibilities, as essential ingredients.

The way that we are using this in our work is through inviting deep conversation, establishing leadership learning circles, individual and group coaching. Our own research into learning and maintaining balance is an ongoing inquiry, with much that we and our clients can discover together. The challenge is to look into the vessel of 'what we don't know that we don't know', to move away from the safe haven of known, stagnating practices. We invite you to join the up-wave, to discover the benefits of a balanced leadership mindset through taking action in a number of ways;

- ▷ By engendering balanced leadership throughout your organisation

- ▷ By becoming more strategic in creating the conditions for success

- ▷ By involving your employees further and by drawing on their qualities and talents, building a stronger workforce

- ▷ By building a culture that better serves the new generation Y

- ▷ By staying ahead of the game on the inclusivity agenda—with balanced leadership.

In so doing, we believe that you, your teams and your organisation will be enormously rewarded.

"It's a question of balance. This is the time for the deep feminine to
emerge as a cocreator of the future with the deep masculine"
Scilla Elworthy (2014, p 130)

REFERENCES

Congram, S. (2013). Dynamic fields of Leadership: a study of underlying social, cultural and collective influences. PhD dissertation. University of Cardiff. http://orca.cf.ac.uk/53524/

Cooper, R. (1976). The Open Field. Human Relations, 29(11), 999-1017.

Elworthy, S. (2014). Pioneering the possible: Awakened leadership for a world that works. California: North Atlantic Books.

Garzema, J., & D'Antonio, M. (2013). The Athena Doctrine. San Francisco: Jossey-Bass.

Goleman, D. (1995). Emotional intelligence. New York: Bantam Books.

Kandola, B. (2009). The value of difference: eliminating bias in organisations. Oxford: Pearn Kandola Publishing.

Kline, N. (2014). Living with time to think. London: Cassell.

Koenig, A. M., Eagly, A. H., Mitchell, A. A., & Ristikari, T. (2011). Are leader stereotypes Masculine? A meta-analysis of three research paradigms. Psychological Bulletin, 137(4), 616-642.

Lewin, K. (1943). Defining the "field at a given time". In D. Cartwright (Ed.), Field theory in social science: selected theoretical papers, Kurt Lewin (pp. 43-59). London: Harper Torchwood.

Mezirow, J. (1991). Transformative dimensions of adult learning. San Francisco: Jossey-Bass.

Sealy, R., & Singh, V. (2008). The importance of role models in the development of leaders' professional identities. In K. Turnbull James & J. Collins (Eds.), Leadership perspectives (pp. 208-222). Basingstoke: Palgraver Macmillan.

Owen, Lord (2014). Creon's fatal flaw-when power corrupts (Nov.) http://www.thepsychologist.org.uk

Scharmer, O. (2009). Theory U: learning from the future as it emerges. San Francisco: Berrett-Koehler.

Williamson, M. (1994). Nelson Mandela, Inaugural Speech.

The following references, which draw on other sources, are the full
quotations of the cuts used within the graphics of each chapter title:

Chapter 3   Success is a science; if you have the conditions,
             you get the result. (Oscar Wilde)

Chapter 4   Leadership is much more an art, a belief, a condition of the
             heart, than a set of things to do. The visible signs of artful
             leadership are expressed, ultimately, in its practice.
             (Max Depree)

Chapter 5   People are like stained-glass windows. They sparkle and
             shine when the sun is out, but when the darkness sets
             in, their true beauty is revealed only if there is a light from
             within. (Elisabeth Kübler-Ross)

Chapter 6   The sun rises each morning to shed light on the things we
             may have overlooked the day before. (Tyler J. Hebert)

Chapter 7   Whilst new leadership approaches are taking into
             consideration the wider field of social interaction,
             the dynamics that underlie social interaction also
             need to be accounted for. (Sue Congram)

Chapter 8   Human resources are like natural resources; they're often
             buried deep. You have to go looking for them, they're not
             just lying around on the surface. You have to create the
             circumstances where they show themselves.
             (Sir Ken Robinson)

Chapter 9   Example is not the main thing in influencing others. It is the
             only thing. (Albert Schweitzer)

Chapter 10   We have a responsibility in our time, as others have had in
             theirs, not to be prisoners of history, but to shape history.
             (Madeleine Albright)

ABOUT THE AUTHORS

Sue Congram, Rosie Mayes and Mary Musselbrook founded Engendering Balance Ltd in 2012 to develop effective leadership practices in which a much broader range of talent is recognised. As directors of the company their pioneering work is already showing how businesses and organisations, large and small, can benefit greatly through illuminating the eclipsed and engendering balanced leadership.

Sue Congram PhD

With thirty years of dedicated practice in consultancy and leadership development, enriched by intense study through my PhD research, I bring a wealth of knowledge and experience to Engendering Balance—to our client work and research, in talks that I give about our ideas and to our publications. My own leadership journey has carved a path in consultancy within both public and private sector organisations, teaching psychology to professionals, as a Board member of a US charity and in writing numerous books and papers. My main passion today is to improve leadership-in-practice. Showing up with my own unapologetic feminine qualities I aim to dispel deeply entrenched myths about leadership and liberate men and women alike in carrying their leadership mantle.

Rosie Mayes

I spent much of my formative life in the international sporting environment, playing netball for England, coaching the Republic of Ireland and Welsh netball teams, working as the sport scientist to the English and Welsh national rugby teams and supporting the development of national, international, Olympic and Paralympic coaches. In a move to help bring the successful principles and practices of elite sport into the corporate world I worked with individuals, teams and organisations to explore how their physical, mental, emotional and spiritual performance needs could be developed in a more balanced way. Engendering Balance enables me to combine my passion for people development with my deep felt desire to significantly influence the leadership landscape of the future.

Mary Musselbrook

Leadership Development has been an exciting and energising focus for my work since my early career as a consultant business psychologist and throughout my roles as change management consultant, employee and organisation development specialist and Human Resources Director. This energy continues to the present day where my work as a consultant, coach and team facilitator brings me into daily contact with mostly inspiring and sometimes frustrating experiences of leadership. The desire to stimulate broader and more expansive thinking about leadership has led to putting Engendering Balance in Leadership at the heart of my commitments. I work across the private, public and not-for-profit sectors with men and women who seek to be part of and influence their leadership culture - creating the conditions for the success of individuals, teams and whole organisations.

INDEX

A

assumptions and beliefs v
attitudes v, 6, 35, 60, 61, 62, 67
author-ing 15
authoritative leadership 33
awareness 26, 27, 33, 35, 36, 54, 55, 58, 59, 60, 62
awareness raising 55, 60

B

balanced leadership vi, viii, 6, 8, 14, 20, 26, 27, 36, 37, 38, 42, 45,
        46, 53, 55, 58, 62, 66, 67, 72
beliefs v, 15, 28, 35, 37, 60, 61, 62
belief systems 42
blame culture 36, 53

C

change management vi, viii, 77
collaboration 16, 24, 26, 34, 37
collaborative leadership 17
collective contribution 12
collective thinking 3
community of practice 45
compassion 24, 43
conditions for success, the 3, 12, 13, 15, 19, 48, 72
conflict-avoidance 7
Congram, Sue 75, 76
connective practices 37
context 3, 13, 19, 24, 42, 47
contradiction 42
culturally established beliefs 28
cultural values 42, 60

D

deep assumptions 26, 60
deference 15
deficit thinking 36

men and women vi, 24, 25, 27, 28, 76, 77
micro-moments 42
Musselbrook, Mary 76, 77
mutual support 17

N

nature-nurture 27

O

organisational community 6, 12, 32, 52
organisational leadership vi, vii

P

performance management systems 32, 45, 59
personal identity 60
personal values 60
positional authority 15
psychological depth 58

Q

qualities of practice viii, 20, 23, 24, 28, 38, 42, 44, 47, 58

R

reflective practice 55, 60
relational and social system 2, 55
relational dynamics 19, 60
relational practices 12
relationship 6, 14, 15, 17, 19, 20, 24, 26, 37, 42, 44, 52, 54
role model learning 66, 67
role modelling 46, 55
role of leader 6

S

self-awareness 60
self-eclipse 34
social and cultural system 4, 6
soft and hard 26
starling qualities 35